THE TWENTIETH CENTURY
JERSEY

RAOUL LEMPRIÈRE

SUTTON PUBLISHING LIMITED

First published in the United Kingdom in 2000 by
Sutton Publishing Limited · Phoenix Mill
Thrupp · Stroud · Gloucestershire · GL5 2BU

British Library Cataloguing in Publication Data
A catalogue record for this book is available from the British Library.

ISBN 0-7509-2688-0

Title page photograph: A cart loaded with seaweed at Le Hocq Common, St Clement, *c.* 1905.

Typeset in 11/14 pt Photina.
Typesetting and origination by
Sutton Publishing Limited.
Printed and bound in England
by J.H. Haynes & Co. Ltd, Sparkford.

Contents

JERSEY: AN INTRODUCTION   5

THE NINETIES LINGER ON   7
1900–9

THE FIRST WORLD WAR: THE END OF AN ERA   23
1910–19

THE TWENTIES   39
1920–9

PRELUDE TO WAR AND OCCUPATION   51
1930–30 JUNE 1940

OCCUPATION AND LIBERATION   79
1 JULY 1940–9 MAY 1945

A NEW BEGINNING   87
1946–59

CHANGING TIMES   99
1960–89

COUNTDOWN TO THE MILLENNIUM   113
1990–2000

ACKNOWLEDGEMENTS AND PICTURE CREDITS   128

A little Jersey town girl in her finery, *c.* 1907. She was born in 1901 and was to live through the greater part of the century and experience the changing times reflected in the pages of this book.

Jersey: An Introduction

In order fully to appreciate and understand the photographs in this book it is necessary to know something about Jersey and its way of life during the twentieth century. The island has an area of 45 square miles, it is the largest of the Channel Islands and the most southerly of the British Isles. It lies in the Bay of Mont St Michel and at the closest point is about 14 miles from the west coast of Normandy. Jersey is a bailiwick comprising the main island and a number of islets, notably the Ecréhous and the Minquiers. The population at the beginning of the twentieth century was 52,576 (1901) and at the end 85,150 (1996). The island is divided into twelve ancient parishes, each of which is an administrative district presided over by a constable (mayor). The capital is the town of St Helier, situated principally in the parish of the same name, approximately halfway along the south coast, but with its suburbs spilling over into neighbouring parishes.

Since 1066, except for a few short breaks, the most recent of which was the German Occupation (1940–5), Jersey has been part of the English (later the British) Dominions. The Sovereign is represented on the island by the Lieutenant Governor. The Chief Magistrate and President of the States Assembly (the legislature) is the Bailiff, before whom in the States, the Royal Court and on special occasions is carried a magnificent silver-gilt mace. It was presented to the island by King Charles II as a proof of his royal affection towards the island where he had been twice received in safety during the Civil War, when he was excluded from the remainder of his realm.

At the beginning of the twentieth century the population was made up of the following: indigenous islanders of Norman descent, and a few of Huguenot descent; a large number of English, Irish and Scots who had come to the island either to set up business or to work; a not inconsiderable number of French hoteliers, shopkeepers and others; and some British 'residents' – retired Navy and Army officers, members of the Indian and Colonial civil service and a few very well-to-do people. As the century advanced this changed considerably. After the Liberation in 1945 more people from mainland Britain settled on the island, including a number of wealthy folk, and the old-time 'residents' gradually died out.

In 1900 the island's prosperity was based on agriculture, tourism and 'the resident'. Agriculture comprised the growing and exporting of potatoes, tomatoes and cattle. This pattern continued up to the German Occupation and resumed after the Liberation, but as time went by the position changed and the growing of broccoli and flowers increased. Today agriculture is not what it was and further diversification has had to take place. The number of herds of Jersey cattle has been greatly reduced and those that remain are much larger than they used to be. Tourism has been steadily declining and many hotels and guesthouses have been closed. Very few rich residents are being admitted. Since the 1970s the finance industry has become far and away the most important on the island and the income that it generates produces the greatest part of the insular revenues. Without the finance industry it would be impossible to sustain the island's economy.

After the Liberation seasonal labour in the agricultural industry was provided by Bretons and for a time Welsh female labour was used for the packing of tomatoes. Those engaged in the work were known as 'the Welsh girls', and some of them married local men and settled on the island. In the hotel and restaurant industry seasonal labour was provided by Italians. Nowadays the workforces in both industries are largely recruited from Madeira and Portugal. The Bretons and the Welsh girls no longer come and most of the Italians departed long ago. Of those Italians who remain, the majority have become the owners or managers of restaurants.

The modes and manners of the islanders have been very similar to those on mainland Britain. However there has been virtually no civil unrest. Crime is worse than it used to be, although not as bad as on mainland Britain, and drugs provide a constant menace. The town of St Helier has not deteriorated like many towns of similar size elsewhere in Britain. A significant problem is the lack of modestly priced accommodation for sale and social housing. There is also concern about the considerable growth of the population.

The prospects for the new millennium are not good. As has been said, the island depends on one industry for the bulk of its revenue and that is one that neither the British Government nor the European Union look upon with much favour. However, in the past the islanders have proved resilient and as one industry failed, another took its place. It is to be hoped that this pattern will be repeated.

The Nineties Linger On
1900–9

The Opera House. It replaced the Theatre Royal, which was destroyed by fire in 1899, and was opened by Lillie Langtry in *The Degenerates* on 9 July 1900. The architect of the new building was Adolphus Curry.

Following the death of Queen Victoria, on 22 January 1901, floral tributes were laid around the base of her statue in the Weighbridge Gardens, St Helier. The statue now stands in the Victoria Park (formerly the Triangle Park) and the gardens have been removed.

The Elementary School, St Mary, built in 1901. Note that the type of school and the entrances for girls and boys are shown in French on the front of the building.

The first Battle of Flowers was held on Victoria Avenue, in honour of the Coronation of King Edward VII and Queen Alexandra, 9 July 1902.

In this animated scene at St Helier's harbour Jersey potatoes are being shipped at the height of the season, *c.* 1903.

The 'White Coons' Banjo Team entry for the Battle of Flowers, 18 August 1904. The group performed in the Triangle Park, and, if wet, in the West Park Pavilion, nicknamed 'The Tin Hut'.

A four-in-hand excursion car progressing through the countryside, *c.* 1905.

The guardhouse and guard at the entrance to Government House, St Saviour's Hill, St Saviour, *c.* 1905.

Carts loaded with seaweed (known locally as *vraic*) at Le Hocq Common, St Clement, *c.* 1905. The Common is now the site of St Clement's parish hall. Over the centuries farmers used huge quantities of seaweed to fertilize the land. This practice was still prominent at the beginning of the twentieth century but by the end had virtually ceased.

Inauguration of the new Shand Mason & Co. horse-drawn steam engine, 31 July 1905. The ceremony took place outside the Town Hall, York Street, St Helier.

The presentation of long service medals to men of the Royal Jersey Militia at a ceremony in the Royal Square, St Helier, 1 October 1905. The medals were presented by the Lieutenant Governor, Major General H.S. Gough CB, CMG.

A group of pupils of the Jersey Ladies' College (now the Jersey College for Girls) with their bicycles, 1905.

Gorey Village station, *c.* 1906. The station, opened in 1873, was originally called Gorey station, being renamed in 1891. A number of national and local advertisements are displayed on the building and along the platform. Above the station to the right may be seen the roof, tower and spire of Gouray church.

Royal Jersey Militia in camp on the slopes of Fort Regent, St Helier, May 1906.

This visit of the band of the French 47th Regiment to the band of the East Surrey Regiment, 23 August 1906.

St Clement's Horticultural Show held at Samarès Manor on 30 August 1906.

Participating bands parading through Cheapside, St Helier, during the Concours Musical, 20 and 21 May 1907.

Mont Orgueil Castle, Gorey, handed over to the States by the Crown on 28 June 1907. This group of dignitaries is seen within the castle walls on that occasion. At their centre is the Lieutenant Governor and the Bailiff. Standing at the rear are the hereditary halberdiers.

Jersey cabbages, c. 1907. The leaves were fed to cattle and other livestock. Sometimes the stalks were dried, varnished and made into walking sticks.

St Helier parish church bazaar and fête held on 23 and 24 September 1908.

The general post office, Halkett Place, St Helier, *c.* June 1909. It was closed when the new post office opened in Broad Street.

The new purpose-built general post office opened in Broad Street, St Helier, on 21 June 1909. The ground–floor entrance and the interior have since been re-modelled.

A beach scene at West Park, St Helier, c. 1909.

A Jersey Eastern Railway train steaming away from Gorey Pier, probably during the 1900s.

The bandstand in the Triangle Park (since renamed Victoria Park), early 1910s. The annual summer concert parties performed here.

A horse-drawn excursion car with a full complement of passengers, 1900s/1910s. The man standing on the right in front of the vehicle is Harry, a well-known guide at that time.

Outside St Clement's parish hall on an election day, early 1900s/1910s. The hall is now known as the Caldwell Hall, and a new parish hall has been built at Le Hocq.

The First World War: The End of an Era 1910–19

Following the death of King Edward VII a procession of dignitaries attended the memorial service, and they are seen here entering St Helier's parish church on 6 May 1910.

The proclamation of the accession of King George V was read in the Royal Square, St Helier, by the Viscount (Sheriff) on 10 May 1910. The plinth is without the statue of King George II, which had been sent away for re-gilding. Here, the crowd is giving 'Three Cheers' for His Majesty.

Major-General Sir Alexander Nelson Rochfort arrives in Jersey to take up his appointment as Lieutenant Governor, June 1910.

A picnic party at Corbière, St Brelade, August 1910.

A typical group of farmers, merchants and others gathered at the Weighbridge ('The Bridge'), St Helier, during the potato season, 1911.

The Coronation of King George V and Queen Mary took place on 22 June 1911. This Norman arch with turrets, at the entrance to the Parade, St Helier, was erected by the Coronation Fêtes Committee and decorated by the Society of Jersey Gardeners to mark the occasion.

The Coronation Fêtes, 22 June 1911. What a goodly display of hats!

The *Roebuck* ran aground on the Kanes Reef, under cliffs on the island's south-west coast, on 19 July 1911.

A 'Paragon' excursion car with a full complement of passengers, on 1 September 1911. It is accompanied by Baker, a well-known guide, who is seen standing in front of the vehicle.

A race from St Malo to Jersey and back was held on 26 August 1912. Four hydro-aeroplanes took part, the first aircraft to arrive in Jersey. Here is one of the entrants at West Park, St Helier.

A crowd in the Royal
Square, St Helier,
welcoming in the New
Year, 31 December
1912.

Jersey Free Church Council's treat for 500 poor children, 2 January 1914.

Jersey District Nursing Association, February 1914. The Very Reverend Samuel Falle, Dean of Jersey, is seen here with some of the ladies who took a great interest in the work of the association.

The Constable of St Helier inspecting vehicles in March 1914. This was a standard procedure when the owners of vehicles desired a renewal of licence. (*Courtesy of Mr I.R. Monins*)

Royal Jersey Militia – C Company, Second Battalion mobilized for active service on 29 July 1914.

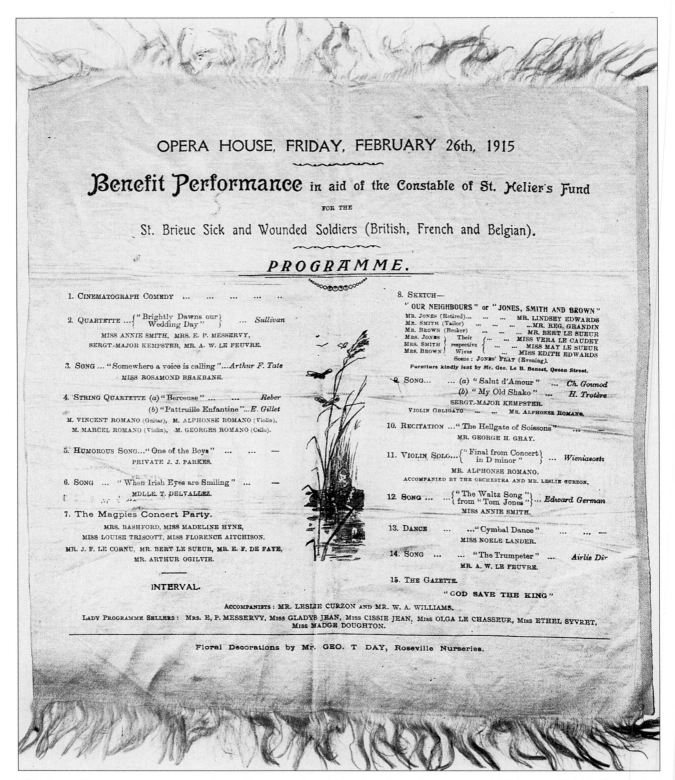

OPERA HOUSE, FRIDAY, FEBRUARY 26th, 1915

Benefit Performance in aid of the Constable of St. Helier's Fund

FOR THE

St. Brieuc Sick and Wounded Soldiers (British, French and Belgian).

PROGRAMME.

1. CINEMATOGRAPH COMEDY ...   .

2. QUARTETTE ...{ "Brightly Dawns our Wedding Day" } ... *Sullivan*
MISS ANNIE SMITH, MRS. E. P. MESSERVY,
SERGT.-MAJOR KEMPSTER, MR. A. W. LE FEUVRE.

3. SONG ... "Somewhere a voice is calling"...*Arthur F. Tate*
MISS ROSAMOND BRAKBANE.

4. STRING QUARTETTE (a) "Berceuse" ...   ...   *Reber*
(b) "Pattruille Enfantine"...*E. Gillet*
M. VINCENT ROMANO (Guitar), M. ALPHONSE ROMANO (Violin),
M. MARCEL ROMANO (Violin), M. GEORGES ROMANO (Cello).

5. HUMOROUS SONG..."One of the Boys" ...   ...   —
PRIVATE J. J. PARKES.

6. SONG   ...   "When Irish Eyes are Smiling" ...   —
MDLLE. T. DELVALLEZ.

7. The Magpies Concert Party.
MRS. BASHFORD, MISS MADELINE HYNE,
MISS LOUISE TRISCOTT, MISS FLORENCE AITCHISON.
MR. J. F. LE CORNU, MR. BERT LE SUEUR, MR. E. F. DE FAYE,
MR. ARTHUR OGILVIE.

INTERVAL.

8. SKETCH—
"OUR NEIGHBOURS" or "JONES, SMITH AND BROWN"
MR. JONES (Retired)...   ...   ...   MR. LINDSEY EDWARDS
MR. SMITH (Tailor)   ...   .MR. REG. GRANDIN
MR. BROWN (Broker)   ...   .MR. BERT LE SUEUR
MRS. JONES } Their { ...   ... MISS VERA LE CAUDEY
MRS. SMITH } respective { ...   ... MISS MAY LE SUEUR
MRS. BROWN } Wives { ...   ... MISS EDITH EDWARDS
Scene : JONES' FLAT (Evening).
Furniture kindly lent by Mr. Geo. Le B. Benest, Queen Street.

9. SONG...   ... (a) " Salut d'Amour "   ...   *Ch. Gounod*
(b) " My Old Shako "   ...   *H. Trotère*
SERGT.-MAJOR KEMPSTER.
VIOLIN OBLIGATO   ...   MR. ALPHONSE ROMANO.

10. RECITATION ..."The Hellgate of Soissons"   ...   —
MR. GEORGE H. GRAY.

11. VIOLIN SOLO...{ "Final from Concert in D minor" } ... *Wieniawski*
MR. ALPHONSE ROMANO.
ACCOMPANIED BY THE ORCHESTRA AND MR. LESLIE CURZON.

12. SONG ...   { "The Waltz Song" from "Tom Jones" }...*Edward German*
MISS ANNIE SMITH.

13. DANCE   ...   ..."Cymbal Dance"   ...   ...   —
MISS NOELE LANDER.

14. SONG ...   ... "The Trumpeter"   ...   *Airlie Dix*
MR. A. W. LE FEUVRE.

15. THE GAZETTE.

" GOD SAVE THE KING "

ACCOMPANISTS : MR. LESLIE CURZON AND MR. W. A. WILLIAMS.
LADY PROGRAMME SELLERS : MRS. E. P. MESSERVY, MISS GLADYS JEAN, MISS CISSIE JEAN, MISS OLGA LE CHASSEUR, MISS ETHEL SYVRET, MISS MADGE DOUGHTON.

Floral Decorations by Mr. GEO. T DAY, Roseville Nurseries.

This Opera House programme printed on silk was produced for a benefit performance on 26 February 1915 held in aid of the Constable of St Helier's Fund for the St Brieuc Sick and Wounded Soldiers (British, French and Belgian).

The German prisoner-of-war camp at Blanches Banques, St Brelade, *c.* 1915–19.

Rear of the funeral procession for Konrad Flechsig, 13 May 1916. Konrad Flechsig was a soldier of the 243rd Infantry Regiment of the German Army, who died at the prisoner-of-war camp at Blanches Banques, St Brelade, on 12 May 1916. This and the following photographs are rare, if not unique. (*Courtesy of Mr H.J. Vibert*)

Eight German soldiers carrying wreaths walk in front of the glass hearse at Konrad Flechsig's funeral, 13 May 1916. (*Courtesy of Mr H.J. Vibert*)

The main body of mourners. The rear of the band, which consisted of sixteen German musicians, is seen in the right-hand corner. (*Courtesy of Mr H.J. Vibert*)

The funeral procession alongside the churchyard of St Brelade's church. The road is lined with men from the Hampshire Regiment with arms reversed. (*Courtesy of Mr H.J. Vibert*)

Here, Konrad Flechsig's funeral procession is seen entering the churchyard of St Brelade's church. (*Courtesy of Mr H.J. Vibert*)

At Flechsig's funeral the coffin was covered with the German flag, with the deceased's service cap resting on the top. The coffin is borne into the church on the shoulders of six soldiers from the 243rd Infantry Regiment. (*Courtesy of Mr H.J. Vibert*)

The Halkett Hotel, St Helier, *c.* 1916. The hotel has been demolished, and the site is now occupied by Morier House, a block of States' offices. (*Courtesy of Mrs J. O'Neil*)

Pupils of the Jersey Ladies' College (now the Jersey College for Girls), *c*. 1916.

Victoria College Officers Training Corps, *c*. 1916.

The erection of this temporary cenotaph at the apex of the Parade Gardens, St Helier, was completed in time for the first anniversary of the end of the First World War, 4 August 1919.

The Twenties
1920–9

An Ann Street Brewery lorry at Caledonia Place, St Helier, in the 1920s.

Gordon Benett's 'Paragon' Car with a
full complement of passengers, 4 June
1920. Standing to the right is Baker, the
well-known guide.

The Opera House in Gloucester Street, St Helier, was severely damaged by fire on 13 May 1921. (*Courtesy of the D.C. Holmes Collection*)

A visit by King George V, Queen Mary and Princess Mary to Jersey, 12 July 1921. The royal party enter St Helier's harbour in a launch from the royal yacht *Victoria and Albert*, moored off Elizabeth Castle. (*Courtesy of the Société Jersiaise Photographic Archive, Jersey*)

42

King George V and Queen Mary on their progress around the island, 12 July 1921. (*Courtesy of Mrs J. O'Neil*)

A proud owner showing off her prize Jersey cow, July 1921.

The Dennis turbine engine and the crew at the fire station, Nelson Street, St Helier, 2 February 1923. The vehicle's solid tyres were replaced by pneumatic tyres in the early 1930s. (*Courtesy of the D.C. Holmes Collection*)

In April 1923 Jersey Motor Transport purchased five Bristol buses with solid tyres. This vehicle is seen at the Weighbridge, St Helier, *c.* 1923. (*Courtesy of Mr Michael Ginns MBE*)

The mailboat *Caesarea* struck a rock off Noirmont on 7 July 1923. Although the boat tried to return to St Helier's harbour, it sank off Elizabeth Castle.

Pioneer No. 2 (later re-named *Portelet*), a Sentinel-Cammell railcar, is seen here standing at the Corbière platform of St Aubin's station, St Brelade, some time between 1924 and 1931.

The Great Western Railway's *St Julien* came into service on the Weymouth–Channel Islands route in May 1925. She was joined later in the year by her sister ship, *St Helier*. Here the *St Julien* is seen on her maiden voyage to Jersey, 24 May 1925.

Primrose Motor Coach Tours' fleet of coaches lined up in Caledonia Place, St Helier, 1926.

St Andrew's Church, First Tower, St Helier, which was opened on 26 September 1927. The architect was C.W. Blanchard Bolton.

Two Sentinel railcars were introduced by the Jersey Eastern Railway in 1927. They were painted red and carried fifty-two second-class passengers each. This railcar, named *Brittany*, is seen on the carriage siding at Snow Hill station, St Helier, some time between 1927 and 1929.

The seaplane *Calcutta* at Jersey, 29 May 1928. The Rt Hon. Sir Samuel Hoare CBE, CMG, MP is being seen off by Major-General The Hon. Sir Francis Bingham, Lieutenant Governor, Lady Bingham and Sir William Venables Vernon KBE, the Bailiff.

Lillie Langtry died on 12 February 1929.
This fine white marble bust stands over her
grave in St Saviour's churchyard.

The Maison St Louis Observatory was demolished on 20 February 1929.

The Militia Ball at Springfield, St Helier, late 1920s/early 1930s. The hall was used for many different purposes, including as a theatre and as a venue for trade shows. It has now been demolished.

Charing Cross, St Helier, with King Street to the left and a glimpse of Broad Street to the right, 1920s/1930s.

Prelude to War and Occupation 1930–30 June 1940

Southern Railway's *Isle of Jersey* came into service on the Southampton–Channel Islands route on 13 March 1930. She was joined by her sister ships, *Isle of Guernsey* and *Isle of Sark*, in 1930 and 1932 respectively.

The world's strongest man pulls a loaded 'Paragon' char-à-banc with his teeth, 2 April 1930. When empty the vehicle weighed 4 tons 15 cwt. (*Courtesy of Mrs J. O'Neil*)

A train leaving St Helier on 24 July 1930 drawn by the locomotive *Corbière*, which was built in 1893.

A Jersey Railway four-compartment first- and second-class bogie passenger carriage at Corbière station, St Brelade, in the final style of livery, 24 July 1930.

A group of holiday-makers outside the Continental Hotel, St Saviour's Road, St Helier, 19 August 1930. The hotel has since been demolished, with flats built on the site.

King Street, St Helier, looking west, *c.* 1931. Woolworth's and Burton's shops remain, but Noel & Porter Ltd, beyond Woolworth's, no longer exists.

West Park Pavilion, designed by architect Roy Charles Blampied, was opened on 1 July 1931. The building is now closed and likely to be demolished.

54

Lightning illuminates St Aubin's Bay during a violent thunderstorm, 28 August 1931.

Firemen of the St Helier's Fire Brigade on church parade, proceeding to Aquila Road Methodist church, St Helier, 29 May 1932. (*Courtesy of the D.C. Holmes Collection*)

A Bristol 'superbus' with its driver at Corbière railway station, St Brelade, 1933. At this time Jersey Motor Transport ran a through-service from Corbière, St Brelade, to St Catherine, St Martin, via St Helier. (*Courtesy of Mr Michael Ginns MBE*)

Southern Railway's *Brittany (III)* made her maiden voyage from Jersey to St Malo on 18 June 1933. In addition to the regular St Malo runs, she also operated day excursions to Guernsey, Alderney and Sark.

The Passenger Air Service to Portsmouth by Jersey Airways started from West Park beach on 18 December 1933. Here a number of the company's aircraft await passengers some time between 1933 and 1937, when the airport at St Peter was opened.

The main shop of Orviss Ltd, grocers, etc., in Beresford Street and Halkett Street, St Helier, *c.* 1934. At the time of this photograph, and for some years afterwards, it was one of the two principal grocers in Jersey. The firm no longer exists. (*Courtesy of Mrs A. Paton*)

The grocery department of Orviss Ltd, where customers would place their orders and wait comfortably seated on the chairs provided, *c.* 1934. (*Courtesy of Mrs A. Paton*)

The provision department of Orviss Ltd, where bacon was sliced to the customer's requirements, *c.* 1934. (*Courtesy of Mrs A. Paton*)

Orviss Ltd at Beresford House, Beresford Street, St Helier, seen here *c.* 1934, was situated almost opposite the main shop. This branch sold confectionery, wines, spirits and tobacco, and hardware at the rear of the premises. (*Courtesy of Mrs A. Paton*)

The confectionery department at Orviss Ltd, Beresford House, Beresford Street, *c.* 1934. (*Courtesy of Mrs A. Paton*)

The greengrocery department of Orviss Ltd, at 22 Beresford Street, St Helier, *c.* 1934. (*Courtesy of Mrs A. Paton*)

The hardware department at Orviss Ltd, *c. 1934.* (*Courtesy of Mrs A. Paton*)

The fish and poultry department at Orviss Ltd, Halkett Street, St Helier, *c.* 1934. It is obviously Christmas-time, which accounts for the splendid display of poultry. (*Courtesy of Mrs A. Paton*)

Orviss Ltd travellers' cars and delivery vans drawn up on Victoria Avenue, beside the Lower Park, St Helier, with Westmount and West Park Pavilion in the background, *c.* 1934. (*Courtesy of Mrs A. Paton*)

St Matthew's Church, Millbrook, St Lawrence, which was rededicated on 29 September 1934. The church was reconstructed in memory of Lord Trent of Nottingham, the founder of Boots the Chemists. The church is notable for its Lalique glass. The architect of the original church was J.T. Parkinson, and A.B. Grayson was the architect during the reconstruction. This view shows the chancel and some of the Lalique glass.

The Font, by René Lalique, at St Matthew's Church, 1934.

Angels by René Lalique at St Matthew's Church.

The Forum Cinema, Grenville Street, St Helier, was opened on 1 March 1935. It was closed in 1981 and demolished in 1984, with blocks of offices being built on the site. (*Courtesy of Mr Roy Heaven*)

The interior of the Forum Cinema, with the Compton Organ in the centre, which is now in Queen's Hall, Fort Regent, St Helier. (*Courtesy of Mr Roy Heaven*)

This archway was erected in York Street, St Helier, by the Royal Jersey Agricultural and Horticultural Society to celebrate the Silver Jubilee of King George V and Queen Mary, 6 May 1935.

For the Silver Jubilee of King George and Queen Mary, on 6 May 1935, this archway was erected by the Battle of Flowers Committee.

The visit of HRH The Prince of Wales on 23 July 1935. He is seen here at Victoria College, accompanied by His Excellency General Sir H. de C. Martelli, the Lieutenant Governor, on his immediate right, and Mr G.H. Grummitt, the Headmaster. (*Courtesy of the Société Jersiaise Photographic Archive, Jersey*)

Mr Alexander Moncrieff Coutanche, the Attorney-General, was appointed Bailiff on 12 August 1934, and sworn in later that month. Here he is seen with Mrs Coutanche in a relaxed mood, *c.* 1938. Mr Coutanche (1892–1973) was Bailiff during the German Occupation and successfully steered the island through those perilous times. He was knighted in 1946 and created a life peer in 1961.

The National Trust for Jersey was founded in August 1936. This is its first property, the 'Don Le Gallais', Vallée-des-Vaux, St Helier, presented by Mr and Mrs Carlyle Le Gallais on 27 June 1937.

The airport at St Peter, opened by Mrs A.M. Coutanche, the Bailiff's wife, on 10 March 1937.

The arch erected in The Parade, St Helier, to celebrate the Coronation of King George VI and Queen Elizabeth, May 1937.

This arch was put up at People's Park, St Helier, for the Coronation of King George VI and Queen Elizabeth, May 1937.

Le Rât Cottage at St Lawrence was the first building acquired by the National Trust for Jersey on 6 November 1937.

The St Helier Fire Brigade –
PE crew in ARP gear on the
forecourt of West Park
Pavilion, St Helier, 1938.
The driver is J. Vautier with
C.O. Remphry beside him;
nearside are H. Pinel and
L. Ledo; offside are W. Patch
and H. Villars. (*Courtesy of
the D.C. Holmes Collection*)

This float, HMS *Jersey*, was entered by the St Helier Agricultural Society in the Parochial Class of the Battle of Flowers, held at Springfield, St Helier, on 26 July 1938. It was complete with working telephone system, siren, signal bell, wireless, movable guns and searchlight. It won first prize.

The Jersey Electricity Company Limited's new showrooms and offices at 11 Broad Street, St Helier, opened by Mr A.M. Coutanche, the Bailiff, on 10 January 1939. The shop front, typical of the period, was remodelled some years ago.

Morel Farm, St Lawrence, presented to the National Trust for Jersey by Mr A.J. Morel on 14 February 1939. This was the first substantial property acquired by the Trust.

The destroyer HMS *Jersey* passing Elizabeth Castle before entering St Helier's harbour on 11 July 1939.

This presentation of gifts to HMS *Jersey* took place at a ceremony at Springfield Showground, St Helier, on 13 July 1939. (*Courtesy of the Société Jersiaise Photographic Archive, Jersey*)

At St Helier's harbour loyal Jerseymen leave to join other British reservists, September 1939.

Mr F.C. Le Gros with his horse at the St Lawrence Agricultural Show, held at St Lawrence Arsenal, in the 1930s. It was the custom at that time for farmers to show their horses at cattle shows. (*Courtesy of Mrs V. Butlin*)

Major A.J. Verini's electric brougham was a familiar sight on the island's roads during the 1930s.

Parade Gardens, St Helier, in the 1930s. Through the trees, now gone, may be seen a group of Gothic Revival buildings flanking the hospital chapel. The architect for these was probably John Hayward. All have since been demolished and an extension to the hospital, incorporating a new chapel, has been built on the site.

A scene from the Jersey Green Room Club's production of *The Gondoliers*, by Gilbert and Sullivan, at the Playhouse Theatre, New Street, St Helier, spring 1940.

Occupation and Liberation 1 July 1940–9 May 1945

German soldiers outside the guard house at the entrance to Government House, St Saviour's Hill, St Saviour, early 1940s. (*Courtesy of the Société Jersiaise Photographic Archive, Jersey*)

German sentry box at College House, Victoria College, St Helier, early 1940s.

Germans and their vehicles at Corbière, St Brelade, early 1940s.

This German staff car is
parked outside the
entrance to St Brelade's
Cemetery, early 1940s.

A German band marches past the West Park Pavilion towards the town, early 1940s. (*Courtesy of the Société Jersiaise Photographic Archive, Jersey*)

German soldiers stand outside the Forum Cinema, Grenville Street, St Helier, between 1940 and 1945. Note that the film being screened at that time was *Victory in the West*. (*Courtesy of the Société Jersiaise Photographic Archive, Jersey*)

A potato inspection, held between 1940 and 1945.

François Marie Scornet was executed by firing squad on 17 March 1941 at St Ouen's Manor. This memorial stone to him is located at the Manor.

AUFRUF
AN DIE BEVOELKERUNG DER INSEL JERSEY

Der Feind Deutschlands steht im Begriff, französischen Boden anzugreifen.

Ich erwarte von der Bevölkerung der Insel Jersey, dass sie unbedingt ruhig bleibt und auch bei Uebergreifen des Kampfes auf die Insel sich jeder feindlichen Haltung und Sabotage gegenüber der deutschen Wehrmacht enthält.

Bei Auftreten der geringsten Anzeichen von Unruhen werde ich die Strassen für jeden Verkehr sperren und Geiseln festnehmen lassen.

Angriffe auf die Wehrmacht werden mit dem Tode bestraft.

Der Kommandant der Festung Jersey,

HEINE,
Oberst.

Jersey, den 6. Juni 1944.

PROCLAMATION
TO THE POPULATION OF THE ISLE OF JERSEY

Germany's enemy is on the point of attacking French soil.

I expect the population of Jersey to keep its head, to remain calm, and to refrain from any acts of sabotage and from hostile acts against the German Forces even should the fighting spread to Jersey.

At the first signs of unrest or trouble I will close the streets to every traffic and will secure hostages.

Attacks against the German Forces will be punished by death.

Der Kommandant der Festung Jersey,

(Signed) HEINE,
Oberst.

Jersey, 6th June, 1944.

Proclamation to the population of the Island of Jersey, 6 June 1944.

This Jersey Motor Transport bus ran on charcoal, seen here in October 1941. Standing by the vehicle, from left to right, are: John (Jack) Tardivel, P.T.A. (Tom) Macready, a French engineer and Major Le Brocq, who managed the company. (*Courtesy of the Société Jersiaise Photographic Archive, Jersey*)

The International Red Cross vessel SS *Vega* in St Helier's harbour, 9 May 1945. (*Courtesy of the Société Jersiaise Photographic Archive, Jersey*)

Liberation Day – crowds outside the Pomme d'Or Hotel, Weighbridge, St Helier, 9 May 1945. (*Courtesy of the Société Jersiaise Photographic Archive, Jersey*)

German prisoners-of-war on the beach opposite Elizabeth Castle preparing to embark on transporters for the United Kingdom, 19 May 1945. (*Courtesy of the Société Jersiaise Photographic Archive, Jersey*)

A New Beginning
1946–59

Mr F.C. Le Gros at the Weighbridge, emptying potatoes from a cental barrel into a sack, 1940s. Note the type of barrel has changed from those seen in previous photographs (see pp. 10, 25). By this time motor lorries had largely replaced the horse-drawn Jersey vans previously used for carrying potatoes. (*Courtesy of Mrs V. Butlin*)

The racing schooner *Westward*, which belonged to T.B. Davis, Jersey's greatest benefactor. After his death it was sunk in Hurd Deep on 15 July 1947, in accordance with his wishes. The vessel is seen here moored in St Helier's harbour some time before the Second World War.

Haystacks being built in the traditional style during the summer of 1948.

A threshing machine at work in the summer of 1948.

International Road Race – the cars line up opposite the West Park Pavilion, St Helier, on 13 July 1950.
(*Courtesy of the Jersey Motor Cycle & Light Car Club*)

Halkett Place, St Helier, viewed from the
southern end looking northwards, *c*. 1950.

Broad Street, St Helier, viewed from east to west, 1952. The general post office, the fourth property along on the left, still retains its original ground-floor frontage.

Breton musicians and folk dancers, Mont Orgueil Castle, Gorey, St Martin, *c.* 1952.

The Postmaster-General unveiled this new postbox in the Parade, St Helier, on 1 December 1952, near the site of one of the first four erected in the British Isles. A plaque affixed to the top of the postbox explains the significance of its location.

This large suspended crown at the junction of Bath Street and Phillip's Street, St Helier, was one of the many decorations displayed to celebrate the Coronation of Queen Elizabeth II on 2 June 1953.

Excavations start at the gas company's property in Tunnell Street, St Helier, c. 1954, in preparation for the building of a vertical retort house, now demolished. This building is seen here during its construction. Megaliths were uncovered during these excavations.

The closing scene of the last night's production of the Jersey Green Room Club's Christmas pantomime *Sinbad the Sailor*, staged at the Forum Cinema, Grenville Street, St Helier, 4 January 1956. (*Courtesy of Mrs D. Lee-Channing*)

HM Queen Elizabeth II presenting the King George V Cup to Mr C.G. Pallot of La Poudretterie, St Martin, on 25 July 1957, the only time that the Cup has been awarded by a reigning monarch. The King George V Cup was originally presented by King Edward VIII in memory of his father, King George V, and is awarded annually for the best animal exhibited in the cattle classes in the Island Spring Show. Mr Pallot's cow, Seers Bouquet, was judged Supreme Champion in the Spring Show held in May. The Cup was handed over at Springfield Showground, St Helier. (*Courtesy of Mr J.G. Pallot*)

Lipscombe the baker's was established in 1811 at 1 Sand Street, St Helier. This photograph from the late 1940s or 1950s shows a shop front full of character. The firm was celebrated for its *vraic* buns, large raisin-filled confections, which were popular with seaweed gatherers.

Samarès post office, Inner Road, St Clement, 1950s. It was opened in 1899 and closed in 1956, although the shop remained open for some time after the closure of the post office.

C.G. Ferbrache, antique and second hand dealer, 34 Hill Street, St Helier, late 1950s/1960s.

East side of Pier Road, St Helier, late 1950s/1960s. The old houses have since been demolished, to be replaced by States' housing.

East side of Pier Road,
St Helier, further down the
thoroughfare, late
1950s/1960s. The first
building on the right was
The Regent, a public house
known to members of the
garrison of Fort Regent as
'The First and Last'.

West side of Pier Road,
St Helier, 1950s/1960s.
Some of these houses
survive, principally as office
accommodation. Others have
been demolished.

A typical scene at St Helier's
harbour during the tomato
season, 1950s/1960s.

Changing Times
1960–89

The Star Restaurant, Wharf Street, St Helier, was the leading restaurant of its day. It is seen here on 25 September 1961, after its closure.

Val de la Mare Reservoir, St Peter, construction of which was completed in 1962. (*Courtesy of The Jersey New Waterworks Co. Ltd*)

Stacks of seaweed (*vraic*) on the sand dunes behind St Ouen's Bay, *c.* 1962. They were sold to farmers at auction.

Queen Elizabeth the Queen Mother walking from the Royal Court to St Helier's parish church, 10 May 1963. The Royal Mace is being carried by Mr H.V. Benest. On the Queen's right is Mr R.H. Le Masurier, the Bailiff, and on her left is General Sir George Erskine, the Lieutenant Governor. (*Courtesy of the Société Jersiaise Photographic Archive, Jersey*)

The visit of Queen Elizabeth the Queen Mother, 10 May 1963. Here she is seen talking with the Very Reverend Alan Stanley Giles, Dean of Jersey, in the churchyard of St Helier's parish church. (*Courtesy of the Société Jersiaise Photographic Archive, Jersey*)

Fort Regent, St Helier, in a state of dereliction in 1964, nothing having been done to it since the Liberation in 1945. It has now been roofed over and converted into a leisure centre.

This fine old granite-built property in Don Street, St Helier, bears the date 1811 and the initials N.W. and A.A. It is seen here in 1964, before its conversion into shops and offices.

St Mary's and St Peter's Church, Vauxhall, St Helier, was refronted in 1965. The church has since been demolished and replaced by a new building in Wellington Road, St Helier. (*Courtesy of Johnson & Johnson of Jersey*)

The small shop on the corner of St Clement's Inner Road and Jambart Lane, opposite St Clement's church, 1965. It was one of many small country shops that became uncompetitive, and were forced out of business by the larger shops and supermarkets.

Simpsons, an old-established stationers, at 9 Library Place, St Helier, is seen here in 1965, after its closure and before demolition.

The bicentenary of the founding of the Jersey Chamber of Commerce, said to be the oldest of its kind in the English-speaking world, was celebrated in 1968. An enlarged reproduction of the Chamber's seal is set into the outside wall of its headquarters in Halkett Place, St Helier.

A float from the Battle of Flowers held on 1 August 1968. It is to be noted that hydrangeas, which were widely used in floats before the Second World War, have been replaced by other flowers.

Church House, Church Street, St Helier, 1969. These premises have been demolished and replaced by a new Church House and a block of offices.

Maison St André, Val Plaisant, St Helier, c. 1969. This fine building was demolished to make way for Convent Court, a block of States' flats.

British Hotel, Broad Street, St Helier, seen here in the 1960s, was one of Jersey's oldest hotels. The premises are now part of a bank.

The first double-decker bus to pass through the tunnel under Fort Regent is seen emerging at the Green Street end, February 1970. The tunnel was opened to traffic on the 25th of that month. (*Courtesy of Mr Michael Ginns MBE*)

The visit of Dr Michael Ramsay, Archbishop of Canterbury, July/August 1970. He is seen here on the right with the Reverend Paul Harrison, Rector of St Clement.

The New Era Cinema, Victoria Road, St Clement, 1972. It was opened in 1952 and closed in 1972.

De Faye's, dispensing chemists, at 21 David Place, St Helier, seen here in 1976. Above the fascia are displayed three coats of arms representing the three royal warrants of appointment granted to the proprietor by Queen Alexandra, Queen Mary and Princess Christian of Denmark respectively.

Gerald Durrell with lowland gorilla Bamenda, spring 1976.
The gorilla was born in Jersey Zoo on 1 October 1975.
Gerald Malcolm Durrell (1925–95) was the founder of Jersey
Zoo and the Jersey Wildlife Preservation Trust (now known
as the Durrell Wildlife Conservation Trust). (*Courtesy of
Mr Philip Coffey*)

High-rise and low-rise at Hue Court, St Helier, built after
1976. The pitched roofs on the low-rise are cosmetic
additions.

This arch was erected at Grouville as part of the celebrations for the Silver Jubilee of HM Queen Elizabeth II, 5 June 1977. The Queen and Prince Philip visited Jersey on 27 June 1978, at the start of their Channel Islands tour.

The Music School, Victoria College, St Helier, completed in September 1977.

Quétivel Mill, which won a Civic Trust Commendation in 1978 and was opened to the public in 1979.

Battle of Flowers, 11 August 1983. Note that the woman and young girl accompanying the float are wearing traditional Jersey sun-bonnets.

The extension to the General Hospital in September 1987, the year that the building was completed. (*Courtesy of Mr R. Briault*)

Countdown to the Millennium 1990–2000

An aerial view of Queen's Valley Reservoir, 29 May 1992. It was completed in 1991. (*Courtesy of Mr R. Briault*)

Jersey Museum, Caledonia Place, St Helier, was completed on 19 March 1992. It was nominated National Heritage Museum of the Year in 1993.

Warehouses that form part of the Jersey Museum complex, completed on 19 March 1992.

Royal Bank House, Bath Street, St Helier, completed in September 1993. It received a Civic Trust Commendation in 1995.

A shop on the corner of Dumaresq Street and Hue Street, St Helier. The delightful old shop and the adjacent properties on Hue Street were restored by Save Jersey's Heritage in 1994.

Properties on the south side of Hue Street, St Helier. They were restored by Save Jersey's Heritage in 1994.

This sculpture was created by Philip Jackson to mark the fiftieth anniversary of the Liberation of the island in 1995. It is situated in Liberation Square, St Helier.

King Street, St Helier, decorated in honour of the fiftieth anniversary of the Liberation, 1995.

117

The Town Hall, York Street, St Helier, decorated in honour of the fiftieth anniversary of the Liberation.

This decorative arch at Grouville was erected in honour of the fiftieth anniversary of the Liberation.

No. 22 Grenville Street, St Helier, on its completion in August 1995. It was designed by architects Susan Garner/The Lobb Partnership. (*Courtesy of Mourant, du Feu & Jeune*)

St Joseph's Church, Grouville. The building was opened in 1895 and closed either late in 1995 or early 1996.

The Occupation Tapestry Gallery, New North Quay, St Helier's harbour, 25 March 1996. The tapestry comprises twelve panels, designed by Wayne Audrain, portraying scenes of the German Occupation. Each of the island's twelve parishes was responsible for making one panel. At the same location is the Maritime Museum, opened on 22 July 1997, which won the National Heritage Museum of the Year award in 1998.

The new departure hall at the airport at St Peter, which was opened in March 1997.

Tributes following the death of Princess Diana on 31 August 1997. On the days after numerous floral tributes were laid on the steps in front of the Royal Court House and at the base of King George II's statue, Royal Square, St Helier.

The Ariadne steam clock outside the east front of the Maritime Museum, which was completed in 1997. It is named after the paddle steamer built in 1824, the first steamship on service between England and the Channel Islands.

La Frégate Café, Waterfront, St Helier, opened on 5 November 1997. It replaced the West Park Café.

Liberté House, La Motte Street, St Helier, opened in 1998.

This clock was installed above the entrance of Rivoli, 41–3 King Street, St Helier, in June 1999. The timepiece was made by John Smith & Son of Derby. The faces revolve and depict, respectively, Agriculture, Tourism and Finance. There is also a special one for Christmas.

Morier House, Halkett Place, St Helier, was
officially opened by HRH The Princess Royal on
23 July 1998. It provides office accommodation
for various States' departments.

Part of a float in the Battle of Flowers held on
12 August 1999.

After being restored and regilded, the statue of King George II was replaced on its plinth in the Royal Square, St Helier, in December 1999. It was originally erected in 1751. The sculptor was John Cheere.

The Millennium Cross, Le Hocq, St Clement, erected in 1999.

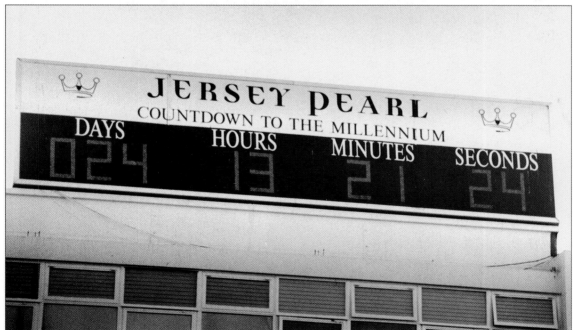

The Millennium Clock above the façade of the bus station in Caledonia Place, St Helier, 1999.

Acknowledgements and Picture Credits

Most of the photographs in this book have come from my own collection and in many cases have been taken by me.

I would like to thank the following people and organizations for permission to reproduce their photographs:

Mr Phillip Coffey; Mr Michael Ginns MBE; Mr Roy Heaven; the D.C. Holmes Collection; the Jersey Motor Cycle and Light Car Club; The Jersey New Waterworks Co. Ltd; Johnson & Johnson of Jersey; Mrs D. Lee-Channing; Mr I.R. Monins; Mourant, du Feu & Jeune; Mrs J. O'Neil; Mr J.G. Pallot; Mrs A. Paton; the Société Jersiaise Photographic Archive, Jersey; Mr H.J. Vibert.

I would also thank the following for their kind assistance: Miss Julia Coutanche and Mr Gareth Syvret of the Société Jersiaise Photographic Archive; Miss Tracy Le Couteur of the Gerald Durrell Wildlife Conservation Trust; Mr David Miller of the States of Jersey Fire Service; Advocate Peter de C. Mourant and Mr J. Phipps of Mourant, du Feu & Jeune; Mr H. Swift, Commercial Manager, Jersey Airport; and Mr Ken Thomson of the Jersey Motor Cycle and Light Car Club.

I am particularly grateful to Mr R. Briault for preparing the photographs for publication and for permitting me to reproduce two of his own; also to Mrs V. Butlin for typing the text and permitting me to reproduce two of her family photographs.

Raoul Lemprière
Jersey, June 2000